Buster Balloon was a giant snail.
He was the biggest balloon for sale.

FOR SALE

Buster was taller than the kangaroo.
Buster was taller than the rabbit, too.

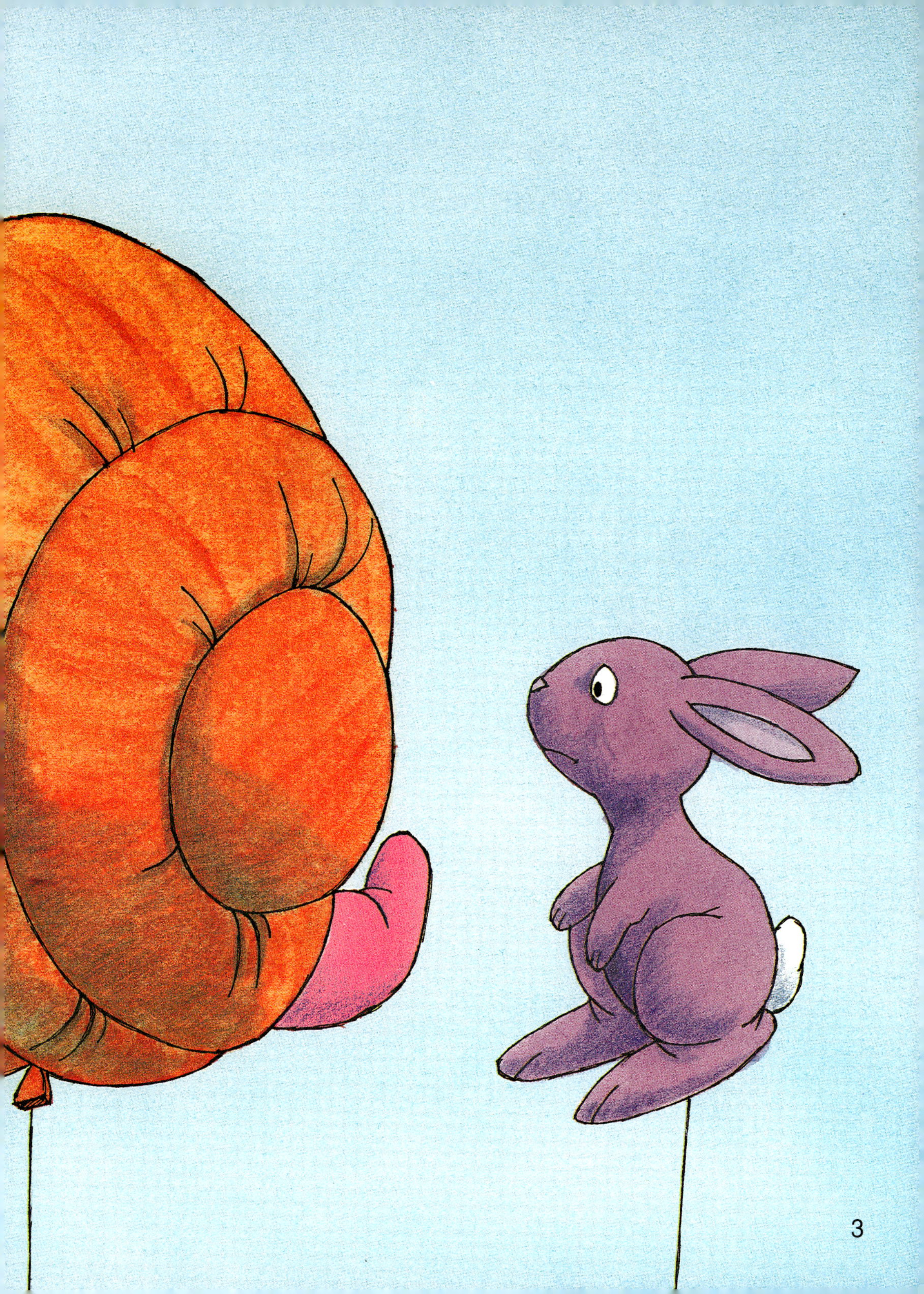

Buster was fatter than the big red rat.
Buster was fatter than the spotty cat.

5

And Buster used to boast all day;
"No one's bigger than me!" he'd say.

7

But one day he began to squeak.
"Oh no!" he said, "I've sprung a leak!"